W9-BWK-653

Title Withdrawn

NOV 05

R
ED
cont.

Issue #2
Fall 2005

biography for beginners

Sketches for Early Readers

Laurie Lanzen Harris,
Editor

Favorable Impressions

P.O. Box 69018
Pleasant Ridge, Michigan 48069

Laurie Lanzen Harris, *Editor and Publisher*
Dan Harris, *Vice President, Marketing*
Favorable Impressions
P.O. Box 69018, Pleasant Ridge, Michigan 48069

ISSN 1081-4973

Printed in the United States

Contents

Preface

Biography for Beginners is a publication designed for young readers ages 6 to 9. It covers the kinds of people young people want to know about—favorite authors, television and sports stars, and world figures.

Biography for Beginners is published two times a year. A one-year subscription includes two 100-page hardbound volumes, published in Spring (May) and Fall (October).

The Plan of the Work

Biography for Beginners is especially created for young readers in a format they can read, understand, and enjoy. Each hardcover issue contains approximately 10 profiles, arranged alphabetically. Each entry provides several illustrations, including photographs of the individual, book covers, illustrations from books, and action shots. Each entry is coded with a symbol that indicates the profession of the person profiled. Boldfaced headings lead readers to information on birth, growing up, school, choosing a career, work life, and home and family. Each entry concludes with an address so that students can write for further information. Web sites are included as available. The length and vocabulary used in each entry, as well as the type size, page size, illustrations, and layout, have been developed with early readers in mind.

Because an early reader's first introduction to biography often comes as part of a unit on a writer like Dr. Seuss, authors are a special focus of *Biography for Beginners*. The authors included in this issue were chosen for their appeal to readers in grades one through four.

There is a broad range of reading abilities in children ages 6 to 9. A book that would appeal to a beginning first-grade reader might not satisfy the needs of an advanced reader finishing the fourth grade. To accommodate the widest range of readers in the age group, *Biography for Beginners* is written at the mid-second grade to third grade reading level. If beginning readers find the content too difficult, the entry could be used as a "read aloud" text, or readers could use the boldfaced headings to focus on parts of a sketch.

Indexes

Each issue of *Biography for Beginners* includes a Name Index, a Subject Index covering occupations and ethnic and minority backgrounds, and a Birthday Index. These indexes cumulate with each issue. The indexes are intended to be used by the young readers themselves, with help from teachers and librarians, and are not as detailed or lengthy as the indexes in works for older children.

Our Advisors

Biography for Beginners was reviewed by an Advisory Board made up of school librarians, public librarians, and reading specialists. Their thoughtful comments and suggestions have been invaluable in developing this publication. Any errors, however, are mine alone. I would like to list the members of the Advisory Board and to thank them again for their efforts.

Gail Beaver   University of Michigan School of Information
                 Ann Arbor, MI

Nancy Bryant   Brookside School Library
                 Cranbrook Educational Community
                 Bloomfield Hills, MI

Linda Carpino   Detroit Public Library
                 Detroit, MI

Helen Gregory   Grosse Pointe Public Library
                 Grosse Pointe, MI

Your Comments Are Welcome

Our goal is to provide accurate, accessible biographical information to early readers. Let us know how you think we're doing. Please write or call me with your comments.

We want to include the people your young readers want to know about. Send me your suggestions to the address below, or to my e-mail address. You can also post suggestions at our website, www.favimp.com. If we include someone you or a young reader suggest, we will send you a free issue, with our compliments, and we'll list your name in the issue in which your suggested profile appears.

And take a look at the next page, where we've listed those libraries and individuals who will be receiving a free copy of this issue for their suggestions.

Acknowledgments

I'd like to thank Mary Ann Stavros for superb design, layout, and typesetting; Catherine Harris for editorial assistance; Barry Puckett for research assistance; and Kevin Hayes for production help.

Laurie Harris
Editor, *Biography for Beginners*
P.O. Box 69018
Pleasant Ridge, MI 48069
e-mail: laurieh@favimp.com
URL: http://www.favimp.com

CONGRATULATIONS!

Congratulations to the following individuals and libraries, who are receiving a free copy of *Biography for Beginners*, Fall 2005, for suggesting people who appear in this issue:

Sister Jeanette Adler, Pine Ridge Elementary, Birdseye, IN

Nancy Margolin, McDougle Elementary, Chapel Hill, NC

Deb Rothaug, Pasadena Elementary, Plainview, NY

Kathy Sinclair, Sabin Elementary, Traverse City, MI

Nancy Vollano, Mathewson Elementary, Milford, CT

Doreen Cronin
1966-
American Author of Books for Children
Creator of *Click, Clack, Moo: Cows That Type*

DOREEN CRONIN WAS BORN in 1966 in the Queens section of New York. Her dad was a policeman and her mom was a homemaker. Doreen has two brothers and a sister.

DOREEN CRONIN GREW UP on Long Island, outside of New York City. She loved to read as a child. Two of her favorite books were *Harold and the Purple Crayon* by Crockett Johnson and *The Stupids* by James Marshall.

DOREEN CRONIN WENT TO SCHOOL at the local schools. After high school, she attended Pennsylvania State University. She majored in journalism.

While at Penn State, she met her first farm animal. She was writing an article about farm life when a cow licked her hand. "I almost fainted," she recalls.

After college, Cronin decided she wanted to become a lawyer. She went to St. John's University law school.

BECOMING A LAWYER: After graduating, Cronin got a job as an attorney. By then, she'd also started to write. The story that eventually became *Click, Clack, Moo* started as an idea way back in college.

STARTING TO WRITE FOR KIDS: Cronin developed the idea for her first book over several years. She sent it off to publishing companies. But she got rejection after rejection. "Like most writers, it took me many years and hundreds of rejection letters before I was fortunate enough to be published," she says. Finally, she found a publisher. And the book went on to be a huge hit.

CLICK, CLACK, MOO: COWS THAT TYPE: As the book's many fans know, *Click, Clack, Moo* features a barnyard full of pretty smart animals. They decide to let Farmer Brown

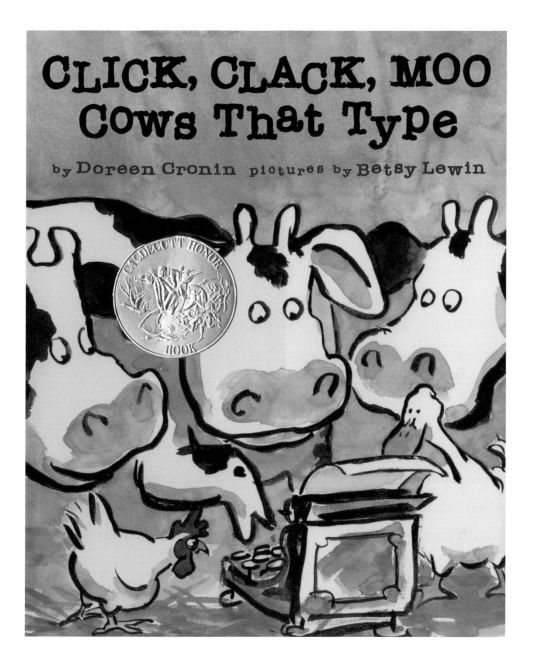

CLICK, CLACK, MOO
Cows That Type

by Doreen Cronin pictures by Betsy Lewin

know just how unhappy they are with life on the farm. The cows get cold at night. They write him a letter to tell him they want electric blankets. He says no, so they say no milk.

The chickens want electric blankets, too. When Farmer Brown says no to them, they stop laying eggs. The problems between the farmer and the animals continue. Duck is the go-between, bringing letters back and forth. Finally, the problems are resolved, and the book comes to a hilarious close — with Duck getting a diving board!

The book has become a favorite with kids and adults alike. The lively illustrations, by Betsy Lewin, help the story come to life. "Betsy's illustrations are, in a word, perfect," says Cronin. Lewin won a Caldecott Honor for the book. That's one of the most important awards in children's book illustration. [See the entry on Betsy Lewin in this issue of *Biography for Beginners.*]

Everyone loves the book's warm humor. Cronin claims that she got her sense of fun from her dad. He passed away several years ago, but his sense of humor lives on. "Whenever someone says that *Click, Clack, Moo* made them laugh, I feel like my Dad is still around cracking people up. I love it," says Cronin.

Cronin became a favorite author, visiting schools across the country. Her young readers were eager for new books. So she decided to quit her job as a lawyer and write full-time.

GIGGLE, GIGGLE, QUACK: Cronin brought back her barnyard crew in *Giggle, Giggle, Quack*. In the book,

Giggle, Giggle, Quack

by Doreen Cronin   pictures by Betsy Lewin

A New York Times
Best-seller

from the creators of CLICK, CLACK, MOO: Cows That Type

Farmer Brown goes on vacation. He leaves the farm in
the care of his brother, Bob. "But keep an eye on Duck,"
Farmer Brown says. "He's trouble."

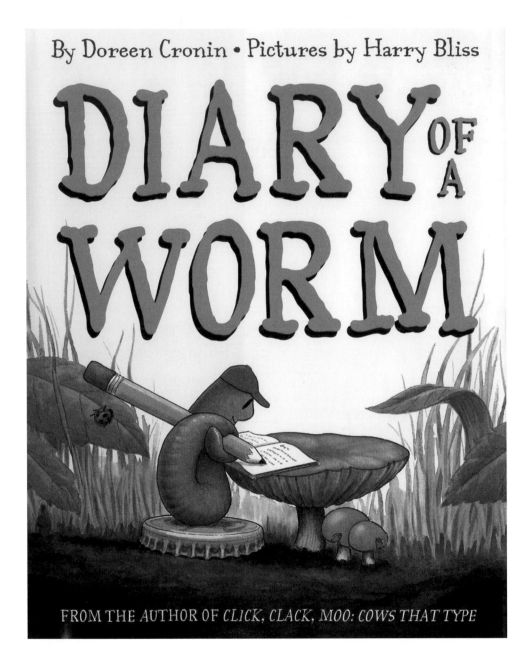

By Doreen Cronin • Pictures by Harry Bliss

DIARY OF A WORM

FROM THE AUTHOR OF *CLICK, CLACK, MOO: COWS THAT TYPE*

Once again, the human characters are duped by the sly, funny animals. Duck, pencil in hand, writes a series of notes for Bob. Bob, thinking the notes are from Farmer Brown, follows the directions exactly. He orders pizza,

gives the pigs a bubble bath, and gets the farmhouse ready for movie night.

Cronin and Lewin once again created an unforgettable book for kids. The two really enjoy working together. They each comment on the other's work, and they sometimes travel to schools and bookstores together, too.

DIARY OF A WORM: Cronin's next book featured another animal — a worm. The book is told in the form of a diary. Following several months in the worm's life, it features stories and pictures of his family and friends. The story follows him as he goes to school, and a dance where he and his fellow worms do the Hokey-Pokey. The wonderful illustrations, by Harry Bliss, feature the little worm, looking a lot like a regular kid.

DUCK FOR PRESIDENT: In 2004, as the U.S. Presidential election rolled around, Cronin returned to the barnyard. This time, Duck is fed up with his job on the farm. He decides to hold an election. He runs against Farmer Brown to become head of the farm. But when he wins, he realizes just how little he likes the job. Next, he runs for governor. But after winning, he discovers that "Running a state is no fun at all."

So Duck sets his sights on the Presidency. In the hilarious conclusion, President Duck finds that life in the White House isn't to his liking. So it's back to the barnyard for him.

Cronin is working on a number of new books. In fact, she says she likes to work on many projects at once. She sometimes bases her characters on people she knows.

One of her most famous characters, Duck, is a lot like her. "Duck is essentially me and every other mischievous child I've ever known and loved," says Cronin.

DOREEN CRONIN'S HOME AND FAMILY: Cronin met her husband, Andrew, in law school. They live in New York with their dog, Ruffie.

Andrew is a lawyer. Cronin says he "goes off to his 14-hour day, while I get to stay home to write or go to visit schools."

Cronin collects antique typewriters — like the kind you see in *Click, Clack, Moo*. But she writes her own books out long hand or on the computer. She is very happy with her life, and doesn't miss being a lawyer at all.

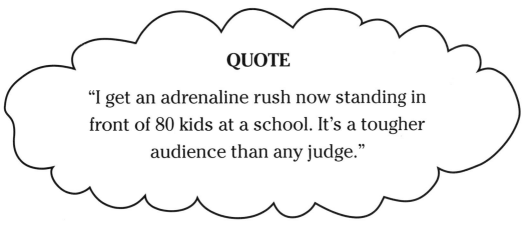

QUOTE

"I get an adrenaline rush now standing in front of 80 kids at a school. It's a tougher audience than any judge."

SOME BOOKS BY DOREEN CRONIN:

Click, Clack, Moo: Cows That Type
Giggle, Giggle, Quack

Diary of a Worm
Duck for President
Diary of a Spider
Wiggle

FOR MORE INFORMATION ABOUT DOREEN CRONIN:

Write: Simon & Schuster Books for Young Readers
1230 Avenue of the Americas
New York, NY 10020

WORLD WIDE WEB SITES:

http://www.childrenslit.com/th_doreencronin.html
http://www.doreencronin.com
http://www.simonsayskids.com
http://www.pippinproperties.com/authill/cronin

Tim Duncan

1976-
American Professional Basketball Player with the San Antonio Spurs
Three-time MVP of the NBA Finals

TIM DUNCAN WAS BORN on April 15, 1976, on the island of St. Croix in the U.S. Virgin Islands. That's an island group in the Caribbean. His full name is Victor Theodore Duncan. His parents were William and Ione Duncan. His father was a hotel owner and also worked for an oil company. His mother was a midwife. That's someone who helps women when they're having babies. Tim has two older sisters named Cheryl and Tricia. He also has three half-brothers, William, John, and Scott.

TIM DUNCAN GREW UP on the beautiful island of St. Croix. It is part of the U.S. Virgin Islands, about 1,000 miles southeast of Florida. The U.S. Virgin Islands are actually part of the U.S., so Tim is a U.S. citizen.

Tim didn't grow up playing basketball. Instead, he started swimming at a very young age. But he didn't swim in the ocean, he swam at a nearby pool. That's because he's always been afraid of sharks.

Tim was an outstanding swimmer, like his older sisters. His sister Tricia was so good that she swam on the U.S. Virgin Islands Olympic team. When Tim was 13, he was one of the best freestyle swimmers in the U.S.

Tim had his sights set on the Olympics, too, until tragedy struck. When he was a teenager, Tim's mom got cancer. She died just before his 14th birthday. Ione had always been her kids' biggest fan, always urging them to do their best. After her death, Tim lost interest in competition.

Another tragedy was in store for the Duncans and all the families on the island. In 1989, Hurricane Hugo hit with such force that it did millions of dollars worth of damage. Homes, businesses, even the pool where Tim swam were destroyed.

TIM DUNCAN WENT TO SCHOOL at the local schools. His Mom had always insisted that her kids do well in school, and Tim did. He was such a good student that he skipped a grade. After his Mom died, Tim still studied hard, and he found a new sport: basketball.

STARTING TO PLAY BASKETBALL: Tim's sister Cheryl married and moved to Ohio. She and her husband sent a basketball hoop to Tim. When they came to visit, Cheryl's husband, a fine player, taught Tim the game. Soon, it became clear that Tim had the talent to become a great player.

Even though he didn't start playing until he was in 9th grade, Tim became a star. He was an outstanding member of St. Dunstan's High School team. And even though few colleges recruit in the U.S. Virgin Islands, Tim got noticed.

COLLEGE BALL: Duncan was offered an athletic scholarship to Wake Forest University. That's a fine school in Winston-Salem, North Carolina. Tim started at Wake Forest in 1993. He was a little shy at first — he'd never lived in a city as big as Winston-Salem. But he got to know the kids, and he loved college.

Duncan playing at Wake Forest.

At Wake Forest, Duncan really came into his own. As a freshman, he was already seven feet tall, and had the skills to be a great center. In his four-year college career, he got better and better. He became one of the finest college players in the country.

Duncan has always been a cool, level-headed player. His teammates at Wake Forest gave him a nickname: "Mr. Spock." That's a character from the old "Star Trek" TV show who shows no emotion.

"It's just how I was brought up," says Duncan. "It's my personality, and it carries onto the court. But I don't see myself as laid back as people say. Once I'm out there, I want to play. I'm excited to play."

Although many basketball stars leave college early to go pro, Duncan wasn't interested. He'd promised his Mom he would finish college, and that's what he did. He graduated from Wake Forest in 1997 with a degree in psychology. Then it was time to consider pro ball and the NBA.

Players join the NBA through a system called the "draft." In the draft, teams choose the players they want. In 1997, Duncan was chosen by the San Antonio Spurs. He was the first player picked.

SAN ANTONIO SPURS: When Duncan joined the Spurs, their star player was David Robinson. He took Duncan under his wing, and the Spurs became the club to beat. In

Number one — Duncan poses after being selected by the San Antonio Spurs as the first pick overall in the 1997 NBA draft.

his first season in the NBA, Duncan helped lead the team to the playoffs. He won NBA Schick Rookie of the Year honors and was the only rookie on the All-Star team.

FIRST NBA CHAMPI-ONSHIP: In the 1998-99 season, Duncan played great basketball. His efforts helped lead the team to the NBA championship. Duncan averaged 27.4 points per game in the final series. His performance earned him MVP honors in the championship.

Duncan had a great season in 1999-2000, but then suffered an injury. He hurt his knee and couldn't play in the playoffs. He'd planned to play on the U.S. Olympic team that year, but he had to sit it out.

Duncan recovered in time to contribute in the next season. The Spurs made it to the quarter finals of the NBA playoffs. In the 2001-2002 season, Duncan really ran up the scoreboard. He put together 2,089 points for the Spurs. That helped win him the league's MVP award for 2002.

SECOND NBA CHAMPIONSHIP: In the 2002-03 season, Duncan shone. Once again, he led the Spurs to the NBA Championship. And once again, he was named the MVP of the finals.

Duncan battles for the ball in the fourth quarter of the seventh game of the NBA finals, June 23, 2005.

In 2004, Duncan played a great season for the Spurs. He also played on the U.S. Olympic team. The team didn't make it to the gold medal round. So Duncan had to settle for third place and a bronze. The gold went to Argentina, featuring his Spurs teammate, Manu Ginobli.

THIRD NBA CHAMPIONSHIP: In the 2004-05 season, Duncan still was the man to go to. He led his team all the way to the finals, where the Spurs battled the Detroit Pistons. Duncan played with two sprained ankles, and the series seesawed back and forth.

Finally, in Game 7, Duncan showed the heart of a champion. He played his best game of the series, leading his team to its third NBA title in just seven years. And for his efforts, Duncan was named MVP of the championship. He's now won the award three times. It places him in very rare company. Only Shaquille O'Neal, Michael Jordan, and Magic Johnson have also won three championship MVPs.

But if you ask him, Duncan says the NBA titles are more important than the MVP awards. "Basketball is a team sport. After you work so hard over the season as a team, what you accomplish together is so rewarding."

With many more years to go in his career, Tim Duncan is at the top of his game. But he's not the type to brag or boast. He just loves to play and be part of his team.

Duncan holding his MVP trophy, left, and the NBA Championship trophy, right, June 23, 2005.

FUTURE PLANS: At the end of the NBA Championship, Duncan was happily making plans for the future. "We just won a championship, and all I'm thinking about is that we could be together for years and play even better."

QUOTE

"I think that basketball and sports in general offer a lot of great lessons to kids.

Dedication: sports require practice, repetition, and hard work.

Teamwork: Basketball is a team sport and working with a team requires patience, selflessness, and compromise.

Camaraderie: Team sports introduce you to all types of personalities and helps you appreciate differences in others and build friendships. Being part of something beyond yourself is powerful."

TIM DUNCAN'S HOME AND FAMILY: Duncan married his college girlfriend, Amy, in 2001. They have a home in San Antonio, which they share with three dogs: Zen, Shadoe, and Nicole.

The Duncans are very active in community charities. Several years ago, they started the Tim Duncan Foundation. They fund programs in education, youth sports, and health. Tim lost both his mom and, a few years ago, his dad to cancer, so he's involved with fundraising to fight the disease. He's also raised funds to build sports facilities for kids in North Carolina and the Virgin Islands. And he donates a block of 40 tickets to each Spurs' home game to charities.

In his spare time, Tim loves to play video games. He also likes movies and the TV show "Alias." He likes to listen to music on and off the court, especially rap, alternative, and reggae.

SOME OF TIM DUNCAN'S RECORDS:

NBA Schick Rookie of the Year: 1998
NBA All-Star: 1998, 2000-2005
NBA Finals Most Valuable Player: 1999, 2003, 2005

FOR MORE INFORMATION ABOUT TIM DUNCAN:

Write: San Antonio Spurs
           One SBC Center
           San Antonio, TX 78219

WORLD WIDE WEB SITES:

http://www.nba.com
http://www.slamduncan.com

Temple Grandin
1947-
American Animal Scientist and Inventor
Creator of Equipment for Humane
Treatment of Livestock
Author of Books on Her Life with Autism

TEMPLE GRANDIN WAS BORN on August 29, 1947, in
Boston, Massachusetts. Her parents are Richard and
Eustacia Grandin. Richard sold real estate and Eustacia
was a singer and actress. Temple is the oldest of four

children. She has two sisters, Isabel and Katherine, and a brother, Richard.

TEMPLE GRANDIN GREW UP in Massachusetts. But she didn't have a regular childhood. When Temple was just six months old, her mother noticed changes in the way she acted. When her mom tried to touch her or pick her up, Temple would stiffen. She hated being touched. It was clear something was wrong.

Temple's parents had her tested by doctors. The doctors told her parents that Temple was autistic.

WHAT IS AUTISM? Autism is a disorder of the nervous system. Doctors aren't sure exactly what causes autism. But they know it has to do with the part of the brain that controls the senses, language, and how we interact with others.

A person with autism is very sensitive to touch, sight, sounds, and smells. They are overwhelmed when their senses are stimulated. That is why Temple couldn't stand to be touched, even as an infant. Instead, she began to withdraw from the everyday world.

Many autistics withdraw so much that they never learn to speak. They also have difficulty understanding relationships. They have trouble "reading" people's emotions.

Temple wanted to be alone. She couldn't speak, and she appeared to be deaf.

She also had terrible temper tantrums. "Loud noise hurt my ears," she remembers. "And I withdrew from touch to avoid overwhelming sensation. My hearing is like having a hearing aid with the volume control stuck on 'super loud'."

When Temple was growing up, very little was known about autism. Most autistic children were sent away from their families, to institutions. But Temple's mother wanted to raise her at home. She did everything she could to make Temple's childhood as normal as possible.

But Temple had a terribly hard time dealing with "normal" life. "I wanted to feel the good feeling of being hugged," she recalls. "But when people hugged me the stimuli washed over me like a tidal wave." Learning to speak was also a huge challenge. "If adults spoke to me, I could understand everything," she says. "But I could not get my words out. It was like a big stutter. My mother and teachers wondered why I screamed. Screaming was the only way I could communicate."

Her mother decided to find a school and a private care giver for Temple. She began daily speech therapy. Her care giver made sure that Temple had plenty to do each day. They played games and did activities with other children. That way, Temple stayed active in the world of other people.

TEMPLE GRANDIN WENT TO SCHOOL at a local private school for normal kids. She was a good student, but had some problems with math. Junior high was more difficult. Temple went to an all-girls private school. Some of the girls were cruel. They said hurtful things, and Temple often lost her temper. She was expelled for throwing a book at a student who called her names.

Temple's next school was the Hampshire Country School. That's a special school for kids who are gifted, and also have emotional problems.

Temple thrived there. She enjoyed her classes, and she spent time horseback riding, which she loved. She had a science teacher in particular who helped her. His name was William Carlock. Mr. Carlock helped Temple understand her autism. He also helped her create a machine to help ease some of her symptoms. It was the "squeeze machine."

FIRST INVENTION — The Squeeze Machine: From the time she was little, Temple knew that she didn't want to be touched. But she also knew that pressure — an all-over squeezing sensation — made her feel more relaxed.

The idea for a "squeeze machine" first came to her when she spent time on her aunt's cattle ranch. At the

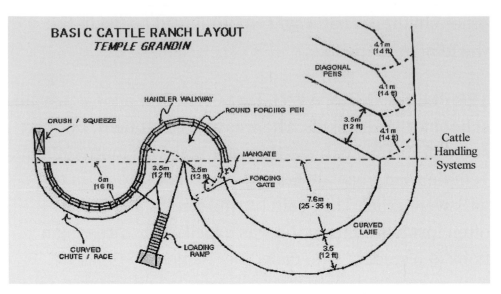

A cattle ranch system designed by Grandin.

ranch, the cattle were placed in a "squeeze chute" when they got their vaccines. The movable sides of the chute would gently press on the cattle's bodies, holding them still as they received their shots. Grandin noticed that the animals relaxed when they were "squeezed."

Temple wanted to try the squeeze chute on herself and see if it helped her anxious feelings. To her great relief, it did.

"For about an hour afterward I felt very calm and serene," she recalls. "My constant anxiety had diminished. This was the first time I ever felt really comfortable in my own skin."

Back at Hampshire, Mr. Carlock helped Grandin build a "squeeze machine" of her own. It worked well, and it helped her enormously. She wasn't as anxious or angry. She did better in school. She got along better with the other kids, too.

The "squeeze machine" became Grandin's first invention. It's helped other children with similar problems. Today it's used to help kids with autism, attention-deficit hyperactivity disorder (ADHD), and other conditions.

Grandin graduated from Hampshire and went to Franklin Pierce College. There, she studied psychology. She did very well, and she also began to develop more social skills. She got to know other students, and felt she fit in.

After graduating from college, Grandin decided to go to graduate school at Arizona State. She'd begun to work with livestock and she wanted to learn more about animals.

BECOMING AN ANIMAL SCIENTIST: Grandin has a deep closeness and understanding of animals. She got a job working a cattle chute. She observed the animals closely. She became "more tuned in to the animals and their feelings of pain and anxiety."

Grandin completed her master's degree in animal sciences. Her special area of interest was animal handling. She went on to work on a PhD. at the University of Illinois in the same subject. She also worked at several jobs in the livestock industry.

"I hardly know what to say about this remarkable book.... It provides a way to understand the many kinds of sentience, human and animal, that adorn the earth."
— Elizabeth Marshall Thomas, author of *The Hidden Life of Dogs*

THINKING IN PICTURES

AND OTHER REPORTS FROM

MY LIFE WITH AUTISM

TEMPLE GRANDIN

WITH A FOREWORD BY OLIVER SACKS

INVENTOR: Grandin started her own company, Grandin Livestock Systems. She began to develop new equipment for handling livestock. She created corrals, pens, chutes, feedlots, and other systems. All of them shared a purpose: to treat livestock humanely.

Grandin's systems have been so successful that one third of the livestock in the U.S. use units she created. The same systems and techniques are used by horse trainers and zoo keepers, too.

"Thinking in Pictures": As an autistic, Grandin processes the world in a unique way. She says that she "thinks in pictures." She designs animal systems in her head, picturing each piece of the process. "I visualize the animal entering the chute from different angles," she says. "Or I turn myself into an animal and feel what it would be like entering the chute."

"Animals are a lot like autistics," she claims. Both "communicate by focusing on the visual. Consider how a whooping crane only has to be shown once how to migrate and they will know it for the rest of their lives."

WRITING AND SPEAKING ABOUT AUTISM: In addition to her work with animals, Grandin has another important role. She has become a spokesperson on autism.

Animals in Translation

Using the Mysteries of Autism to Decode Animal Behavior

"Deeply moving and fascinating."
—Oliver Sacks

Temple Grandin and Catherine Johnson
author of **Thinking in Pictures**

Grandin is one of the first people with autism to write about it. And she's one of the first people to talk about autism from an *autistic* point of view. She's written several books and gives many speeches every year. She talks to parents, scientists, and others interested in autism. She shares with them the techniques that helped her learn to communicate and succeed. She helps parents help their children, and teachers help their students. She hopes to continue her work for years to come.

QUOTE

"The reason the autistic child shuts out the world is because it hurts. And if you let the child shut out the world, his brain won't develop. You have to keep forcing them to interact. You've got to keep playing little games with them to get them to interact with you. It helps the nervous system to hear and see better."

TEMPLE GRANDIN'S HOME AND FAMILY: Grandin lives in a townhouse in Fort Collins, Colorado. She's a professor of animal behavior at Colorado State University. She isn't married and doesn't have children. She decided long ago that it would be very difficult to form those kinds of relationships. Instead, she focuses on her work with animals and autism. "My work is my life," she says.

FOR MORE INFORMATION ABOUT TEMPLE GRANDIN:

Write: Grandin Livestock Systems
2918 Silver Plume Drive C-3
Fort Collins, CO 80526

WORLD WIDE WEB SITES:

http://www.grandin.com
http://www.templegrandin.org

Freddie Highmore
1992-
English Actor and Star of *Charlie and the Chocolate Factory*

FREDDIE HIGHMORE WAS BORN on June 9, 1992, in London, England. His parents are Edward and Sue Highmore. Edward is an actor and Sue is an agent who helps actors find roles.

FREDDIE HIGHMORE IS GROWING UP in a family where acting is part of family life. His parents want him to have

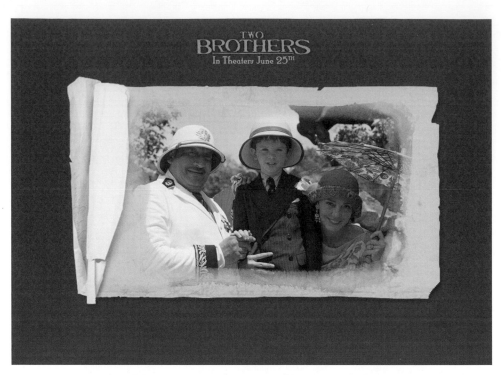

Freddie in a poster for Two Brothers.

a normal childhood, though. Freddie has lots of friends and activities outside of acting.

STARTING TO MAKE MOVIES: Freddie appeared in his first movie when he was six. He also was featured in several TV movies from the ages of seven to 10. These included *Happy Birthday Shakespeare* and *The Mists of Avalon.* In *The Mists of Avalon,* he played King Arthur as a little boy.

Freddie's next TV movie was *Jack and the Beanstalk: The Real Story.* In it, he got the chance to act with his dad, Edward.

Freddie's next movie was *Two Brothers*. In that film, he played a boy named Raoul who gets a tiger cub. The cub has become separated from its brother. The movie is about how the "two brothers" find each other again.

FINDING NEVERLAND: Freddie's first major role was in *Finding Neverland*. That movie is about J.M. Barrie, who created Peter Pan. Freddie plays Peter Llewelyn Davies. He was Barrie's inspiration for Peter Pan.

Freddie played in the movie with stars Johnny Depp and Kate Winslet. The two adult actors were amazed at

Highmore as Peter Llewelyn Davies in a scene with Johnny Depp in Finding Neverland.

Freddie's abilities. "He was astonishingly good and pure and sweet" said Depp. Winslet said that Freddie was the finest child actor she'd ever worked with. "He is something else. I would literally get hairs up on the back of my neck watching him act."

Freddie became very close to Depp. When Depp's next movie was announced, Freddie wanted to be part of it. Based on Depp's and Winslet's recommendations, Freddie got the role. He got to play Charlie Bucket in *Charlie and the Chocolate Factory*. The movie made him a star.

CHARLIE AND THE CHOCOLATE FACTORY: The film came out in the summer of 2005. Kids and adults both loved it.

The movie is based on a book by Roald Dahl. Freddie had read the book, but he didn't want to see the earlier film version. "I thought it was better to wait until afterwards," he said. "I thought I ought to create my Charlie on my own."

Charlie is one of five children chosen to visit the famous, mysterious Willie Wonka and his amazing chocolate factory. When the children arrive, they're in for a fabulous — and unusual — adventure.

The movie was directed by Tim Burton. Freddie said it was a great experience working with him. "Tim Burton managed to bring out Roald Dahl's imagination," he said.

Highmore as Charlie Bucket in Charlie and the Chocolate Factory.

According to Freddie, the movie sets were fabulous. "The chocolate room was good. There was a 50-foot waterfall and a boat going down the river. It was really a bit overwhelming. The first thing that struck me was just the size of it."

Many kids wonder if Freddie is like Charlie. "I think we're similar in some ways," says Freddie. "At the end of *Finding Neverland* I was quite upset and I wished to see Johnny again. Charlie has a wish to go to the factory. And both of our wishes came true. Also, I'm just a normal kid and Charlie's just a normal kid."

FREDDIE HIGHMORE GOES TO SCHOOL at a local school near his London home. He says his school friends don't treat him differently because he's an actor.

FUTURE PLANS: Freddie has several new movies coming out in the next year. One is called *The Awful End* and another is *Arthur and the Minimoys*. He hasn't decided whether he'll keep acting when he grows up.

QUOTE

"There are just so many other things I want to do. I haven't fully made up my mind because I love acting. But I really want to go traveling in South America, as well as doing lots of other things."

FREDDIE HIGHMORE'S HOME AND FAMILY: When he's not working, Freddie lives with his mom and dad in London. In his spare time he likes to play soccer (he calls it "football") with his friends. His favorite team is Arsenal. Freddie also likes to play video games.

SOME OF FREDDIE HIGHMORE'S MOVIES:

Two Brothers
Finding Neverland
Charlie and the Chocolate Factory

FOR MORE INFORMATION ABOUT FREDDIE HIGHMORE:

Write: Warner Bros.
4000 Warner Blvd.
Burbank, CA 91522

WORLD WIDE WEB SITE:

http://chocolatefactorymovie.warnerbros.com/about/
cast_highmore

Betsy Lewin
1937-

Ted Lewin
1935-
American Authors and Illustrators of Children's Books

BETSY LEWIN WAS BORN on May 12, 1937, in Clearfield, Pennsylvania. "Lewin" became her last name when she married. Her name when she was born was Betsy Reilly. Her parents were John and Winifred Reilly. John sold

insurance and Winifred was a kindergarten teacher. Betsy
has an older brother.

BETSY LEWIN GREW UP in Pennsylvania loving to draw.
She drew all over everything—blank pages in books,
napkins, and the sidewalk. She also loved to be outside,
close to animals and nature. She had relatives who had a
farm, and she spent a lot of time there, too. She especially
liked to ride horses.

Betsy's mom was a kindergarten teacher, and she read
to her kids every night. Betsy remembers hearing and
loving *Winnie the Pooh, Babar*, and Beatrix Potter's books.
Betsy's dad was a wonderful storyteller. Together, her
parents raised Betsy to love books, words, and stories.

BETSY LEWIN WENT TO SCHOOL at the local public
schools. She was always known as the "class artist." Her
friends used to ask her to draw things for them. "Draw
me a monkey," "Draw me a pig," "Draw *me*," they'd say.
They were delighted with the results.

Betsy's parents and teachers always encouraged her.
Her high school didn't offer art classes, so she studied
with a local artist. When she finished high school, she
knew she wanted to go to art school. Her parents wanted
her to go to a traditional college. But Betsy won out, and
went to Pratt Institute. That's a fine art school in New
York City.

At Pratt, Betsy received excellent training in many art styles. "I just jumped in with both feet and struggled for years and years," she says. While at Pratt, she met her future husband, Ted Lewin.

They liked each other immediately. "He showed me a picture of his pet lion cub, and that did it," Betsy recalls. "We realized that we were both interested in travel. We wanted to go to Africa to see the great herds before they dwindled. And we laughed together. We just had so much in common." They married in 1963.

FIRST JOBS: After graduation, Betsy got a job with a greeting card company. She said that she got to decide "where to put the sparkles on the Christmas cards." After working for the company for a while, Betsy decided she wanted to freelance. She continued to create greeting cards, but she started to write for kids, too.

STARTING TO WRITE FOR CHILDREN: Betsy began to write and illustrate stories for a children's magazine called "Humpty Dumpty." A children's book editor saw her poem, "Cat Count," and loved it. She suggested that Betsy develop the poem into a book. She did, and she found what she wanted to do for the rest of her life.

"I loved the idea of telling a story in a sequence of pictures," she recalled. "I thought, 'Well, I've really found where I belong."

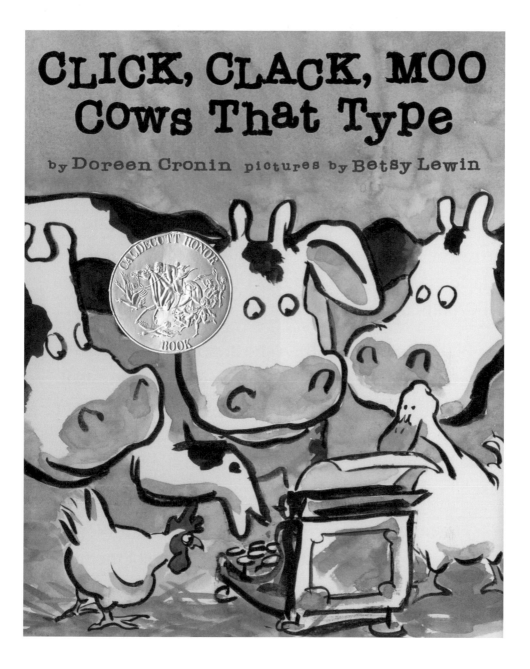

BETSY LEWIN'S BOOKS: In the past 40 years, Betsy Lewin has written and illustrated works of her own, and also illustrated for other authors. One of the books she's written and illustrated is *Booby Hatch*. It's about a bird called a booby. His name is Pepe, and he lives on the Galapagos Islands. That book was inspired by Betsy's travels to those islands off the coast of South America. Another of her books is *Walk a Green Path.* It features plants from around the world.

ILLUSTRATING FOR OTHER AUTHORS — *CLICK, CLACK, MOO: COWS THAT TYPE*: Betsy Lewin is probably best known today as the illustrator of the hilarious *Click, Clack, Moo* by Doreen Cronin. [See entry on Cronin in this issue.]

Betsy remembers when she first received the story. "I just couldn't stop laughing long enough to illustrate it," she recalls. Illustrating the book was a breeze. "I never did a book so fast in my life," she says. "The pictures just came into my mind so quickly and onto the paper so fast."

The book was a terrific success. The illustrations won Lewin her first Caldecott Honor. That's one of the highest awards in children's book illustration. Betsy has illustrated two more books in the series. *Giggle, Giggle, Quack* and *Duck for President* bring the barnyard gang back for more adventures.

Lewin says that she and Cronin work very well together. They give each other ideas, and they've become good friends, too.

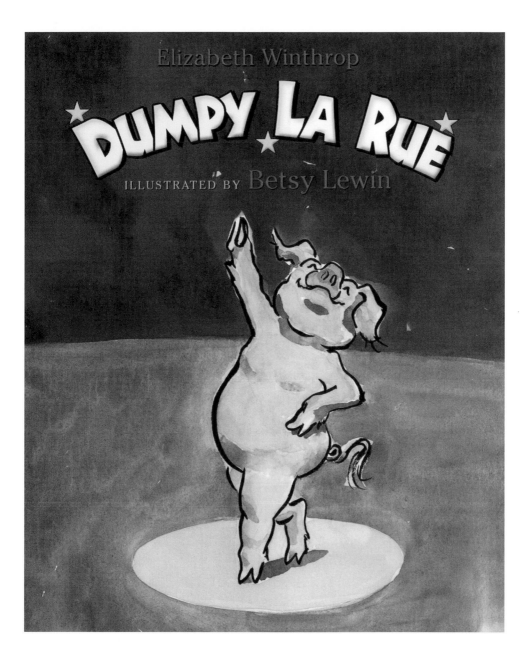

Betsy has illustrated many other books, too. Two favorites are *Araminta's Paintbox* and *Dumpy LaRue*. She's also created several successful books with her husband, Ted.

TED LEWIN WAS BORN on May 6, 1935, in Buffalo, New York. His parents were Sidney and Bernece Lewin. Sidney was a jeweler and Bernece was a homemaker. Ted had two brothers and one sister.

TED LEWIN GREW UP in a house that included, besides his family, "a lion, an iguana, a chimpanzee, and an assortment of more conventional pets." The lion had been given to his brother Donn, who was a pro wrestler. Eventually, his mom convinced Donn to give the cub to the local zoo.

This remarkable household was perfect for Ted. His family always encouraged his love of everything from animals to art. "I always wanted to be an illustrator," he recalled. "As a kid I spent endless hours by myself drawing and copying the work of artists I admired." He especially loved the art of N.C. Wyeth, Winslow Homer, and John Singer Sargent.

Ted read his brother's *Tarzan* books, and copied out all the illustrations. These books of adventure, along with his love of animals and nature, influenced his future career.

TED LEWIN WENT TO SCHOOL at the local public schools in Buffalo. After high school, he attended Pratt Institute in New York City. But he paid for college in a rather unusual way.

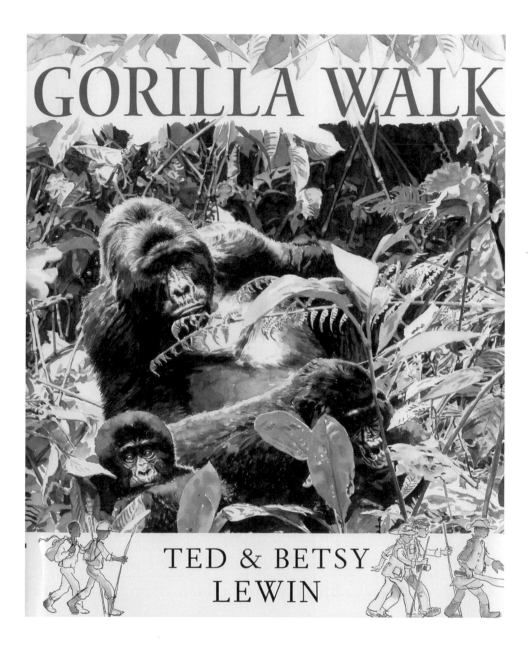

BECOMING A PROFESSIONAL WRESTLER: The Lewin family had always enjoyed pro wrestling. His brother Donn had become a pro wrestler in the 1940s. When Ted was a teenager, he began to wrestle in pro matches on the weekends. The money was good enough that it paid for art school.

Even after art school, Ted continued to wrestle. It helped pay the bills as he got himself established as an artist. He wrote about that life in his autobiography, *I Was a Teenage Professional Wrestler.*

STARTING TO ILLUSTRATE BOOKS FOR CHILDREN: After college, Ted started getting work as an illustrator. He illustrated adventure books, then began to get assignments creating children's book art. He's worked steadily for more than 40 years. He writes and illustrates his own books, illustrates books for other authors, and also creates books with his wife, Betsy.

WRITING AND ILLUSTRATING HIS OWN WORK: Ted has always loved animals and travel. When he and Betsy first visited Africa, it changed his life. He decided to try to put into words and pictures what he'd experienced. "My first picture book, *Faithful Elephants,* gave me the chance not only to draw animals but to make a strong statement about man's cruelty to them in certain circumstances."

Ted has always made sure that his young readers understand how animals in the wild are threatened by man. Often, their habitats are taken away by humans for farm land. Sometimes they are hunted almost to extinction. These are the stories he tells in his books.

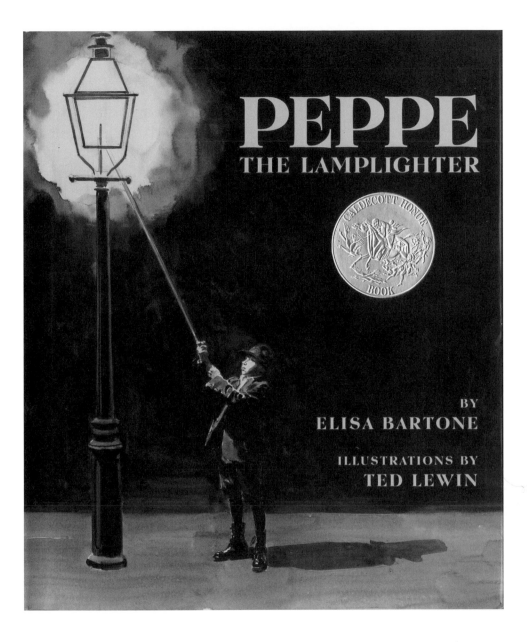

"I realized that the picture book was the best possible world for an illustrator, and I've devoted my full time to it ever since." Many of his books are based on his travels around the world. His concern for preserving wildlife

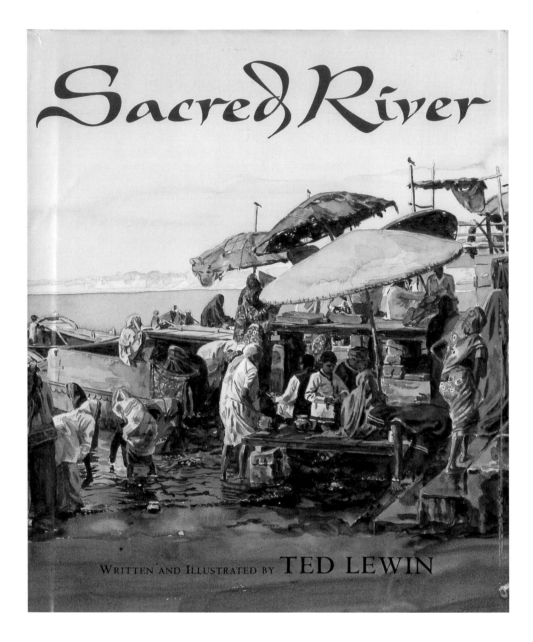

inspired his *World within a World* series. Titles in the series include books on the Everglades and Baja California.

Ted and Betsy's trip to India inspired *Tiger Trek* and *Sacred River*. After visiting Brazil, he wrote *Amazon Boy* and *When the Rivers Go Home.* In *The Reindeer People* he recounts his trip to Lapland.

BOOKS FOR OTHER AUTHORS: Ted has illustrated many books for other authors, too. Among his finest is *Peppe the Lamplighter*, which won a Caldecott Honor. The book, written by Elisa Bartone, features a little boy in old New York who lights the lamps in his Italian neighborhood.

BETSY AND TED LEWIN'S BOOKS: The Lewins have spent the last 40 years writing and illustrating books individually. Recently, they've begun creating books together.

The books they do together have grown out of their love of nature, animals, and travel. Their first book, *Gorilla Walk,* is about their trip to Uganda. In that mountainous African nation, they hiked up slippery paths to find mountain gorillas. They spent hours hiking, then looking for the gorillas. It was hard, exhausting work. But then they found the gorillas, and it was all worth it.

On the plane home, they talked about their incredible experiences. They decided it would make the perfect story to tell together. Betsy remembers how they divided up the work. "I would do the field sketches of us tripping and falling through the jungle, running out of water, and looking tired. At one point, Ted actually slid down the mountain and was stopped by our guide. I could do sketches from memory. And when we finally got to see the gorillas, Ted would do the big family portraits. And it worked out really well."

Their second book together is *Elephant Quest.* That book chronicles their trip to the delta region of Botswana. Their third book is about traveling to Australia. It's called *Top to Bottom: Down Under.* The Lewins have many other ideas, and hope to continue creating books together for years to come.

QUOTE

Betsy

"I love writing and illustrating for children. It's hard to say which I like best, writing and illustrating my own books, or illustrating books by other authors. Journeying to a new place and finding a story to tell from the treasure chest of new experiences there, is always exciting and deeply satisfying. The first time I read a manuscript written by another author I feel all the excitement and anticipation of unwrapping a present. I welcome the challenge of illuminating that author's words with my pictures."

BETSY AND TED LEWIN'S HOME AND FAMILY: Betsy
and Ted Lewin live in a big brownstone in Brooklyn, New
York. They don't have children, but they share their
home with two cats.

Ted's studio is on the top floor, and Betsy's is on the second floor. They get up early every morning and work alone in their studios for several hours.

"We work pretty much in silence from seven o-clock in the morning until about one o'clock," Betsy says. They'll pass on the stairs and chat. "Come up and see what I'm doing," Ted says to Betsy. "No, I was up there last time. You come down here and see what I'm doing," she tells him. "An illustrator's life is really pretty much a hermit's life,"says Betsy. "You sit in your own studio, and you work in silence for however many hours you can stand it."

The Lewins still take wonderful trips all over the world to do research for their books. Whether doing books together or individually, they love their work.

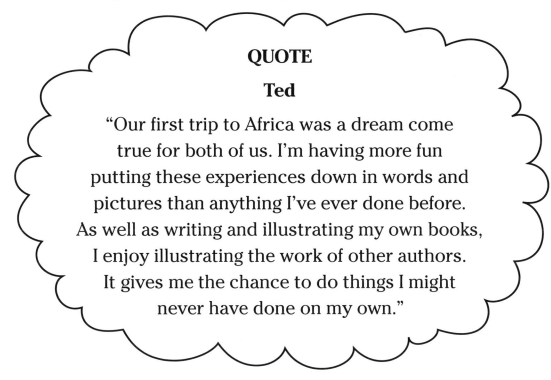

QUOTE

Ted

"Our first trip to Africa was a dream come true for both of us. I'm having more fun putting these experiences down in words and pictures than anything I've ever done before. As well as writing and illustrating my own books, I enjoy illustrating the work of other authors. It gives me the chance to do things I might never have done on my own."

SOME BOOKS BY BETSY LEWIN

As Author and Illustrator

Animal Snackers
Cat Count
Booby Hatch
Walk a Green Path
Groundhog Day

As Illustrator

Kitten in Trouble
Araminta's Paintbox
Jim Hedgehog and the Lonesome Tower
First Grade Elves
Ho! Ho! Ho! The Complete Book of Christmas Words
Mattie's Little Possum Pet
Somebody Catch My Homework
YO! Hungry Wolf: A Nursery Rap
What's Black and White and Came to Visit?
My Tooth is about to Fall Out
First Grade Friends
Two Eggs, Please
Click, Clack, Moo: Cows That Type
Giggle, Giggle, Quack
Duck for President

SOME BOOKS BY TED LEWIN

As Author and Illustrator

World within a World: Everglades

World within a World: Baja
World within a World: Prilofs
Faithful Elephants
Tiger Trek
When the Rivers Go Home
Amazon Boy
I Was a Teenage Professional Wrestler
The Reindeer People
Sacred River
America Too
Market!
Fair!
Touch and Go: Travels of a Children's Book
Nilo and the Tortoise
Red Legs: A Drummer Boy of the Civil War
Tooth and Claw: Animal Adventures in the Wild

As Illustrator

The Cheese Stands Alone
Earthquake
Zia
Patooie
Mama
Soup for President
Hub
National Velvet
Mother Teresa
The Serpent Never Sleeps

Island of the Blue Dolphins
Bird Watch
The Day of Ahmed's Secret
Peppe the Lamplighter
Cowboy Country
The Always Prayer Shawl

SOME BOOKS BY BETSY AND TED LEWIN

Gorilla Walk
Elephant Quest
Top to Bottom: Down Under

FOR MORE INFORMATION ABOUT
BETSY AND TED LEWIN:

Write: HarperCollins Children's Books
1350 Sixth Ave.
New York, NY 10019

WORLD WIDE WEB SITES:

http://www.betsylewin.com
http://www.harperchildrens.com
http://www.nccil.org/blewin.html
http://www.tedlewin.com

Danica Patrick

1982-
American Race Car Driver
First Woman to Lead at the Indianapolis 500

DANICA PATRICK WAS BORN on March 25, 1982, in Beloit, Wisconsin. Her parents are T.J. and Bev Patrick. T.J. owns a glass company and Bev manages a restaurant. Danica has one younger sister, Brooke.

DANICA PATRICK GREW UP in Roscoe, Illinois. Her mom says she was a real "girlie girl" growing up. "She didn't want to get grease under her fingernails," says Bev Patrick.

STARTING TO RACE: That all changed when Danica was 10 and started to race go-karts. It was originally her sister Brooke's idea. "I didn't want to be left out," says Danica. "So I said, 'Sure, I'll do it, too'."

On her first drive, she crashed into a wall when her brakes failed. But she wasn't scared. She couldn't wait to race again. She worked hard at it, and she got better and better. "As I slowly got faster and faster, and then started winning races, I got hooked."

She took racing very seriously. Her dad, who used to race midget-cars, was her coach. He taught her all about how an engine works. So she learned a lot about cars and racing. And she loved to compete. "I might finish a second and a half ahead of everyone," she says. "But it was never good enough."

Danica started winning local races, then competed regionally. By the time she was 12, she was a national champion. Soon she was ready to move on to cars with real speed.

DANICA PATRICK WENT TO SCHOOL at the local public schools in Roscoe. She enjoyed school and activities like band, choir, and cheerleading. But soon racing became the center of her life.

MOVING TO EUROPE: When she was just 16, Danica left her family and moved to England. She knew she wanted to be a professional racer, so she left school to follow her dreams. (She finished her high school degree several years later.)

In England, Danica began racing "formula cars." That's a type of high-speed racing car. There are many different kinds of "formula cars." Each type is determined by the size of the car and the engine, and the amount of power the engine can produce.

LIFE AS A RACE CAR DRIVER: Danica spent three years on the European race circuit. It was sometimes lonely. She often stayed with friends and slept on couches. But she was doing what she loved. And she was learning fast.

Danica placed second in the 2000 Formula Ford race. It was the best finish ever by an American, male or female. The racing world took notice. Bobby Rahal, a former racing champion, offered her a spot on his team. TV great David Letterman is also a co-owner of the team.

In 2002, Patrick signed a long-term contract with the Rahal Letterman team. She returned to the U.S. In 2003 she began racing in the Toyota-Atlantic series. That year,

Patrick in her Indy car.

she had five finishes in the top-five. In one race, she became the first female ever to finish in the top three.

In 2004, Patrick finished third in the Toyota-Atlantic Championship. More importantly, she was chosen to represent Rahal Letterman in the Indy Car series. That meant she would race in the Indianapolis 500.

THE INDIANAPOLIS 500: The Indianapolis 500 is the most famous competition in racing. Drivers spend their entire careers hoping to qualify, and dreaming of winning, at Indy.

Patrick was only the fourth woman ever to qualify. The other three are Janet Guthrie, Lyn St. James, and Sarah Fisher. And of all four, Patrick had the best chance to win it. Her average speed at the time trials was 227 miles per hour. On the day before the race, she clocked the fastest time of all drivers.

On the day of the race, Patrick faced a huge amount of pressure. But she drove like the champion she is, right into the history books. In front of 300,000 spectators and millions more watching on TV, she became the first woman ever to lead at the Indy 500.

The Indy 500 is a long, hard race. It's 500 miles, at speeds well over 200 miles per hour. It's a difficult track, and there's always accidents. At one point, Patrick ran into another car, crushing her car's nose cone. She headed into the pits. Just 60 seconds later, her car was repaired, and she was back in the race.

Patrick led for a total of 19 laps, then ran low on fuel. As the race drew to a close, three other cars passed her, and she finished fourth. It had been an amazing race. She had both led the field, and finished better than any woman, ever. "If I could have run full fuel . . . " she said when it was over. "We'll never know. But I'd like to think we could have maybe won it."

After her awesome finish, fans wanted to know every-thing about her. Some seem more interested in how she looks than in her racing ability. But Danica wants to be taken seriously as a driver. "In the end it boils down to speed," she says. Her boss, Bobby Rahal, tells people not

to focus on how she looks. "Underneath she is as tough as steel," he says.

ARE RACE CAR DRIVERS ATHLETES? Many people wonder whether race car drivers like Danica are real athletes. "It's a very difficult sport," she claims. "They've done tests on drivers, and their heart rate can stay at 180 beats per minute for two hours. Every time you turn the wheel side to side, you can feel everything from your neck and shoulders down to your lower back working."

Patrick trains every day. Her workouts include running, yoga, and weight lifting. She's petite—just 5'1" and

100 pounds. But she's very strong. And she's incredibly competitive. "If I'm doing something, it's because I feel I can beat everyone," she says.

And like other great athletes, Danica has special abilities. Like soccer great Mia Hamm, she can look at a fast-moving situation in slow-time. She can analyze it, and make decisions, while the action's going on around her. "When we're going 200-plus mph, I can see things happening and have time to react to them. I think that is a special gift."

FUTURE PLANS: Danica plans to keep racing for years. "I race because it's fun, and I race because I love it. Racing is the one sport where men and women compete on a level playing field. As Lyn St. James once told me, 'The car doesn't know if you're a man or a woman'."

DANICA PATRICK'S HOME AND FAMILY: Danica lives in Phoenix, Arizona. She's engaged to a physical therapist named Paul Hospenthal. Paul calls her "the most focused person I've ever met in my life."

To relax, Danica likes to listen to music. She says she likes "everything but country and classical." She likes movies, too, especially comedies.

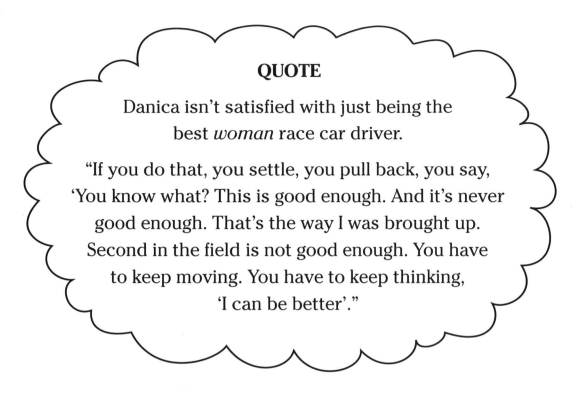

QUOTE

Danica isn't satisfied with just being the best *woman* race car driver.

"If you do that, you settle, you pull back, you say, 'You know what? This is good enough. And it's never good enough. That's the way I was brought up. Second in the field is not good enough. You have to keep moving. You have to keep thinking, 'I can be better'."

FOR MORE INFORMATION ABOUT DANICA PATRICK:

Write: Rahal Letterman Racing
4601 Lyman Dr.
Hilliard, OH 43026

WORLD WIDE WEB SITES:

http://www.danicaracing.com
http://www.rahal.com/drivers/patrick/

Brian Pinkney

1961-
American Author and Illustrator of
Children's Books
Author and Illustrator of *Max Found Two Sticks*
Illustrator of *Alvin Ailey* and *Duke Ellington*

BRIAN PINKNEY WAS BORN on August 28, 1961, in
Boston, Massachusetts. His parents are Jerry and Gloria
Pinkney. Jerry is an artist and illustrator, and Gloria is an
author. Brian was the second of four kids. He has an older

sister named Troy, and two younger brothers, Scott and Myles. Brian was named for his dad, so his full name is "Jerry Brian Pinkney." He's known as "Brian."

BRIAN PINKNEY GREW UP in a family that loved and celebrated art. The kids all played musical instruments, and there were always art supplies around.

Brian remembers spending time at the Elma Lewis Center for the Arts in Boston. "It's where I was first exposed to music, dance, art, and drama," he says. "It's where I first became interested in playing the drums." All his life, he's loved drums. He still plays them and collects them, too.

When Brian was nine, his family moved to New York. By then, he knew he wanted to be an artist, like his dad. [You can read more about Jerry Pinkney in *Biography for Beginners*, Spring 2002.]

"I wanted to be just like him," he remembers. "I did everything he did. My desk was a miniature of his desk. The paintbrushes and pencils I used were often the ones from his studio that were too old or too small for him to use. I had a paint set like his and a studio just like his. Except my studio was a walk-in closet, which made it the perfect size for me."

BRIAN PINKNEY WENT TO SCHOOL at the local schools in Massachusetts and New York. For extra credit, he illustrated his school papers. Brian also loved playing drums and taking tae kwon do. After high school, he attended the Philadelphia College of Art. He studied illustration. After graduating, he worked for a while, then went to graduate school. He got his master's from the School of Visual Arts in New York City.

FIRST JOBS: Pinkney got a job at *Field and Stream* magazine after college. He worked as an art assistant. He also got to know a certain staff member named Andrea Davis. He and Andrea fell in love and got married. Andrea Davis Pinkney is now the author of many beloved children's books. Many of these are illustrated by Brian. [You can read more about Andrea Davis Pinkney in *Biography for Beginners*, Fall 2004.]

BECOMING A CHILDREN'S ILLUSTRATOR: Brian began illustrating children's books in the 1980s. Some of his best-known work appears in books written by Robert San Souci. These include *Sukey and the Mermaid, The Faithful Friend,* and *Cendrillon.* Many of these books offer retellings of African-American folk tales.

Many of Pinkney's books are based on stories from African-American history. It is very important to him to create books that feature stories for and about African-Americans. He's illustrated books about famous black

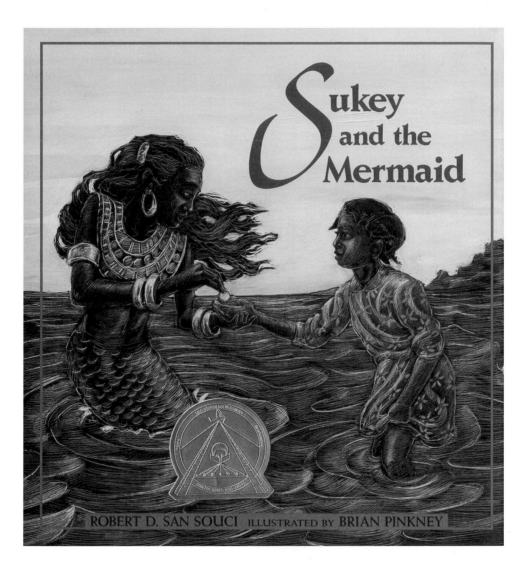

Americans, including Harriet Tubman, Martin Luther King, and Ella Fitzgerald. "I like illustrating stories about African-American subjects," he says. "I learn about my culture and heritage."

WRITING AND ILLUSTRATING HIS OWN BOOKS:
Pinkney has also written and illustrated books of his own.

Some of these have grown out of his hobbies and other interests. "For *Max Found Two Sticks*, I remembered what it felt like to play the drums for the first time," he says.

"When I wrote *Jojo's Flying Side Kick* I recalled the feeling I had as a beginner in tae kwon do."

ILLUSTRATING BOOKS WRITTEN BY ANDREA DAVIS PINKNEY: Brian has illustrated many books by many authors. But his illustrations for books written by his wife, Andrea Davis Pinkney, are special. Many feature the achievements of famous African-Americans.

ALVIN AILEY: The first book they did together was *Alvin Ailey*. It is a biography of a famous African-American dancer and choreographer. (A choreographer is someone who creates dances.) Andrea always does a lot of research for her books. For this first book, she took classes with Ailey's dancers. Brian took the classes, too. He also observed the dancers to make sure he got them just right.

DUKE ELLINGTON: Another favorite book by the Pinkneys is *Duke Ellington*. It features the life of one of the greatest composers of the 20th century. Ellington created a new kind of music. He wrote some of the greatest songs, and created one of the greatest bands, of the era. While creating the illustrations, Brian listened to Ellington's music. He watched movies of the musician, to capture the way he looked and moved.

Andrea's writing and Brian's art form a beautiful tribute to this legend. *Duke Ellington* received a Caldecott

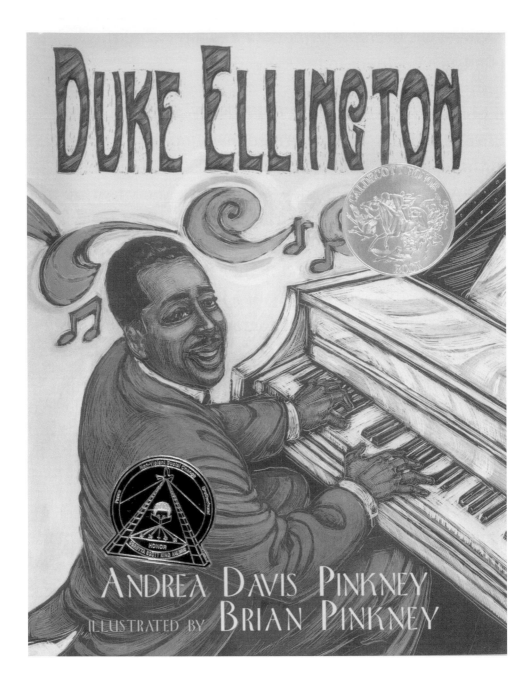

Honor in 1999. That's one of the highest awards in children's book illustration.

The Pinkneys have also created books for toddlers. Some are board books, like *Pretty Brown Face* and *Shake Shake Shake*, for little folks to enjoy.

HIS ARTWORK: Brian uses a special technique, called "scratchboard," for his illustrations. He begins with a white board, covered in black ink. Then he scratches out his drawings using a sharp tool. When that's done, he adds color. He uses watercolors, oils, and acrylics.

"Working in scratchboard is like drawing, etching, and sculpting all at the same time," he says. His pictures are rich with color. They bring characters to life on the page.

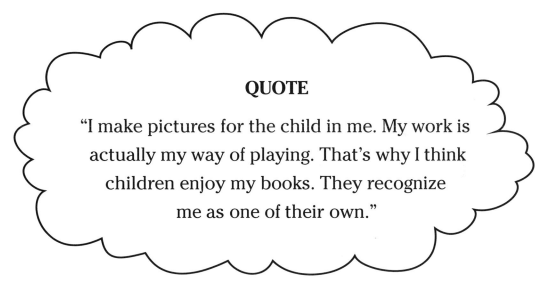

QUOTE

"I make pictures for the child in me. My work is actually my way of playing. That's why I think children enjoy my books. They recognize me as one of their own."

BRIAN PINKNEY'S HOME AND FAMILY: Brian met his wife, Andrea, while working in New York. They married in 1991 and have two children, Chloe and Dobbin. They live in Brooklyn.

In his spare time, Brian still loves to play the drums. He likes all kinds of music, especially jazz. He says if he weren't an artist, he'd be a jazz drummer.

SOME BOOKS BY BRIAN PINKNEY

As Author and Illustrator

Max Found Two Sticks
Jojo's Flying Side Kick
The Adventures of a Sparrow
Cosmo and the Robot

As Illustrator

The Boy and the Ghost
Sukey and the Mermaid
Cut from the Same Cloth
The Faithful Friend
Cendrillon: A Creole Cinderella
Harriet Tubman and Black History
Where Does This Trail Lead?
The Dark-thirty: Southern Tales of the Supernatural
The Elephant's Wrestling Match
Seven Candles for Kwanzaa*
Dear Benjamin Banneker*
The Dream Keeper and Other Poems
Day of Delight: A Jewish Sabbath in Ethiopia
I Left My Village
Bill Pickett, Rodeo Ridin' Cowboy*
Pretty Brown Face*

*I Smell Honey**

*Watch Me Dance**

*Duke Ellington**

*Ella Fitzgerald**

*Written by Andrea Davis Pinkney

FOR MORE INFORMATION ABOUT BRIAN PINKNEY:

Write: Houghton Mifflin Children's Books
222 Berkeley St.
Boston, MA 02116

WORLD WIDE WEB SITES:

http://www.eduplace.com/kids/hmr05/mtai/bpinkney
http://www.hyperionbooksforchildren.com/authors/
http://www.simonsays.com

Photo and Illustrations Credits

Doreen Cronin/Photo: Simon & Schuster Books. Covers: CLICK, CLACK, MOO: COWS THAT TYPE (Simon & Schuster Books for Young Readers) Jacket illustrations copyright © 2000 by Betsy Lewin. Jacket design by Anahid Hamparian; GIGGLE, GIGGLE, QUACK (Simon & Schuster Books for Young Readers) Jacket illustrations copyright © 2002 by Betsy Lewin. Jacket design by Anahid Hamparian; DIARY OF A WORM (Joanna Cotler Books/An imprint of HarperCollins Publishers) Jacket art © 2003 by Harry Bliss. Jacket design by Alicia Mikles; DUCK FOR PRESIDENT (Simon & Schuster Books for Young Readers) Jacket illustrations copyright © 2004 by Betsy Lewin. Jacket design by Dan Potash.

Tim Duncan/Photos: Copyright 2005 NBAE. Nathaniel S. Butler/NBAE via Getty Images; Doug Pensiger/Getty Images; AP/Wide World Photos; AP/Eric Gay/Wide World Photos; AP/M. Spencer Green/Wide World Photos.

Temple Grandin/Photos: Copyright © Laura Wilson; Courtesy of Temple Grandin. Cover: THINKING IN PICTURES Copyright © 1995 by Temple Grandin. Vintage/A division of Random House, Inc.; ANIMALS IN TRANSLATION Jacket photograph by Jason Fulford. Copyright © 2005 Simon & Schuster Inc.

Freddie Highmore/Photos: © 2005 Warner Bros. Entertainment Inc.; © 2004 Universal Pictures; Miramax Films; © 2005 Warner Bros. Entertainment Inc.

Betsy and Ted Lewin/Photo: HarperCollins Publishers. Covers: DUMPY LA RUE (Henry Holt and Company, LLC) Jacket illustration © 2001 by Betsy Lewin; GORILLA WALK (Lothrop, Lee & Shepard Books) Jacket illustrations © 1999 by Ted and Betsy Lewin; PEPPE THE LAMPLIGHTER (Lothrop, Lee & Shepard Books) Jacket illustration © 1993 by Ted Lewin; SACRED RIVER (Clarion Books) Jacket illustration copyright © 1995 by Ted Lewin; ELEPHANT QUEST (HarperCollins Publishers) Jacket arts © 2000 by Ted and Betsy Lewin.

Danica Patrick/Photos: Jonathan Ferrey/Getty Images; Gavin Lawrence/Getty Images; AP/Terry Renna/Wide World Photos.

Brian Pinkney/Photos: Hyperion. Covers: SUKEY AND THE MERMAID (Four Winds Press/Macmillan Publishing Company) Jacket illustrayion copyright © 1992 by Brian Pinkney; MAX FOUND TWO STICKS (Aladdin Paperbacks/Simon & Schuster) Copyright © 1994 by Brian Pinkney; DUKE ELLINGTON text copyright © 1998 by Andrea Davis Pinkney. Illustrations copyright © 1998 by Brian Pinkney; ALVIN AILEY text copyright © 1993 by Andrea Davis Pinkney. Illustrations copyright © 1993 by Brian Pinkney.

Name Index

Listed below are the names of all individuals who have appeared in *Biography for Beginners,* followed by the issue and year in which they appear.

Subject Index

This index includes subjects, occupations, and ethnic and minority origins for individuals who have appeared in *Biography for Beginners.*

Suzuki, Ichiro, Fall 2003

Swoopes, Sheryl,
  Spring 2000

Van Dyken, Amy,
  Spring 2000

Vick, Michael, Spring 2003

Wie, Michelle, Spring 2004

Williams, Serena, Fall 2003

Woods, Tiger, Fall '98

Yamaguchi, Kristi, Fall '97

Austrian

Bemelmans, Ludwig,
  Spring 2004

Australian

Fox, Mem, Fall 2004

Irwin, Steve, Spring 2003

authors

Aliki, Spring '96

Applegate, K.A.,
  Spring 2000

Avi, Spring 2003

Bemelmans, Ludwig,
  Spring 2004

Berenstain, Jan, Fall '95

Berenstain, Stan, Fall, '95

Blume, Judy, Fall '95

Brett, Jan, Spring '95

Bridwell, Norman, Fall '99

Brown, Marc, Spring '98

Bunting, Eve, Fall 2001

Burton, Virginia Lee,
  Spring '97

Byars, Betsy, Fall 2002

Cannon, Janell, Spring '99

Carle, Eric, Spring '95

Carson, Ben, Fall 2003

Christopher, Matt, Fall '97

Cleary, Beverly, Spring '95

Clements, Andrew,
  Spring 2005

Cole, Joanna, Fall '95

Cooney, Barbara,
  Spring 2001

Crews, Donald, Fall '99

Cronin, Doreen, Fall 2005

Curtis, Christopher Paul,
  Spring 2000

Dahl, Roald, Fall 2000

Danziger, Paula, Fall 2001

Delton, Judy, Spring 2004

dePaola, Tomie, Spring '98

DiCamillo, Kate, Spring
  2005

Ehlert, Lois, Fall 2000

Ellerbee, Linda, Fall 2003

Falconer, Ian, Fall 2003

Fox, Mem, Fall 2004

Giff, Patricia Reilly,
  Spring 2001

Grandin, Temple, Fall 2005

Vice President of the United States

Birthday Index

January

12 John Lasseter (1957)
14 Shannon Lucid (1943)
17 Shari Lewis (1934)
21 Hakeem Olajuwon (1963)
26 Vince Carter (1977)
28 Wayne Gretzky (1961)
29 Bill Peet (1915)
Rosemary Wells (1943)
Oprah Winfrey (1954)
30 Dick Cheney (1941)

February

4 Rosa Parks (1913)
7 Laura Ingalls Wilder (1867)
9 Wilson "Snowflake" Bentley (1865)
11 Jane Yolen (1939)
Brandy (1979)
12 Judy Blume (1938)
David Small (1945)
13 Mary GrandPré (1954)
15 Norman Bridwell (1928)
Amy Van Dyken (1973)
16 LeVar Burton (1957)
17 Michael Jordan (1963)
22 Steve Irwin (1962)
27 Chelsea Clinton (1980)

March

2 Dr. Seuss (1904)
David Satcher (1941)
3 Patricia MacLachlan (1938)
Jackie Joyner-Kersee (1962)
4 Garrett Morgan (1877)
Dav Pilkey (1966)
5 Mem Fox (1946)
Jake Lloyd (1989)
8 Robert Sabuda (1965)
10 Shannon Miller (1977)
11 Ezra Jack Keats (1916)
12 Virginia Hamilton (1936)
15 Ruth Bader Ginsburg (1933)
16 Shaquille O'Neal (1972)
17 Mia Hamm (1972)
18 Bonnie Blair (1964)
20 Fred Rogers (1928)
Lois Lowry (1937)
Louis Sachar (1954)
21 Rosie O'Donnell (1962)
25 DiCamillo, Kate (1964)
Sheryl Swoopes (1971)
Danica Patrick (1982)
31 Al Gore (1948)

April

3 Jane Goodall (1934)
    Amanda Bynes (1986)
5 Colin Powell (1937)
7 RondeBarber (1975)
    Tiki Barber (1975)
8 Kofi Annan (1938)
12 Beverly Cleary (1916)
    Tony Hawk (1968)
15 Tim Duncan (1976)
    Emma Watson (1990)
16 Garth Williams (1912)
18 Melissa Joan Hart
    (1976)
26 Patricia Reilly Giff
    (1935)
27 Ludwig Bemelmans
    (1898)
    Barbara Park (1947)

May

4 Don Wood (1945)
6 Judy Delton (1931)
    Ted Lewin (1935)
10 Leo Lionni (1910)
    Christopher Paul
      Curtis (1953)
    Ellen Ochoa (1958)
11 Peter Sis (1949)
12 Betsy Lewin (1937)
14 George Lucas (1944)
    Emmitt Smith (1969)

17 Gary Paulsen (1939)
20 Mary Pope Osborne
    (1949)
22 Arnold Lobel (1933)
29 Andrew Clements
    (1949)

June

2 Freddy Adu (1989)
5 Richard Scarry (1919)
6 Cynthia Rylant (1954)
7 Larisa Oleynik (1981)
9 Freddie Highmore
    (1992)
10 Maurice Sendak (1928)
    Tara Lipinski (1982)
11 Joe Montana (1956)
13 Tim Allen (1953)
15 Jack Horner (1946)
18 Chris Van Allsburg
    (1949)
25 Eric Carle (1929)
26 Nancy Willard (1936)
    Derek Jeter (1974)
    Michael Vick (1980)
30 Robert Ballard (1971)

July

2 Dave Thomas (1932)
6 George W. Bush (1946)
7 Michelle Kwan (1980)
11 E.B. White (1899)
    Patricia Polacco (1944)

July (continued)

12 Kristi Yamaguchi
(1972)
14 Peggy Parish (1927)
Laura Numeroff (1953)
18 Nelson Mandela (1918)
24 Barry Bonds (1964)
Mara Wilson (1987)
26 Jan Berenstain (1923)
28 Beatrix Potter (1866)
Jim Davis (1945)
31 J.K. Rowling (1965)
Daniel Radcliffe (1989)

August

2 Betsy Byars (1928)
3 Tom Brady (1977)
4 Jeff Gordon (1971)
6 Barbara Cooney (1917)
David Robinson (1965)
9 Patricia McKissack
(1944)
Whitney Houston
(1963)
11 Joanna Cole (1944)
12 Walter Dean Myers
(1937)
Fredrick McKissack
(1939)
Ann M. Martin (1955)
15 Linda Ellerbee (1944)
16 Matt Christopher
(1917)

18 Paula Danziger (1944)
19 Bill Clinton (1946)
21 Stephen Hillenburg
(1961)
23 Kobe Bryant (1978)
24 Cal Ripken Jr. (1960)
26 Mother Teresa (1910)
27 Alexandra Nechita
(1985)
28 Brian Pinkney (1961)
29 Temple Grandin (1947)
30 Virginia Lee Burton
(1909)
Sylvia Earle (1935)
Donald Crews (1938)
31 Itzhak Perlman (1945)

September

1 Gloria Estefan (1958)
3 Aliki (1929)
7 Briana Scurry (1971)
8 Jack Prelutsky (1940)
Jon Scieszka (1954)
Jonathan Taylor
Thomas (1982)
15 McCloskey, Robert
(1914)
Tomie dePaola (1934)
16 Roald Dahl (1916)
18 Ben Carson (1951)
Lance Armstrong
(1971)
24 Jim Henson (1936)

September (continued)

- **25** Andrea Davis Pinkney (1963)
- **25** Will Smith (1968)
- **26** Serena Williams (1981)
- **28** Hilary Duff (1987)
- **29** Stan Berenstain (1923)
- **30** Dominique Moceanu (1981)

October

- **1** Mark McGwire (1963)
- **5** Grant Hill (1972)
  Maya Lin (1959)
- **6** Lonnie Johnson (1949)
- **7** Yo-Yo Ma (1955)
- **8** Faith Ringgold (1930)
- **9** Zachery Ty Bryan (1981)
- **10** James Marshall (1942)
- **11** Michelle Wie (1989)
- **12** Marion Jones (1975)
- **13** Nancy Kerrigan (1969)
- **17** Mae Jemison (1954)
  Nick Cannon (1980)
- **18** Wynton Marsalis (1961)
- **22** Ichiro Suzuki (1973)
- **23** Pele (1940)
- **25** Pedro Martinez (1971)
- **26** Hillary Clinton (1947)
  Steven Kellogg (1941)
  Eric Rohmann (1957)
- **28** Bill Gates (1955)

November

- **3** Janell Cannon (1957)
- **4** Laura Bush (1946)
- **9** Lois Ehlert (1934)
- **12** Sammy Sosa (1968)
- **14** Astrid Lindgren (1907)
  William Steig (1907)
  Condoleezza Rice (1954)
- **15** Daniel Pinkwater (1941)
- **19** Savion Glover (1973)
  Kerri Strug (1977)
- **21** Ken Griffey Jr. (1969)
- **25** Marc Brown (1946)
- **26** Charles Schulz (1922)
- **27** Bill Nye (1955)
  Kevin Henkes (1960)
  Jaleel White (1977)

December

- **1** Jan Brett (1949)
- **5** Frankie Muniz (1985)
- **10** Raven (1985)
- **18** Christina Aguilera (1980)
- **19** Eve Bunting (1928)
- **22** Jerry Pinkney (1939)
- **23** Avi (1937)
- **26** Susan Butcher (1954)
- **30** Mercer Mayer (1943)
  Tiger Woods (1975)